Can't Fight the Feelings

RICHARD ▼ DUNN

VICTOR BOOKS
A DIVISION OF SCRIPTURE PRESS PUBLICATIONS INC.
USA CANADA ENGLAND

ABOUT THE AUTHOR

RICHARD DUNN is Chairman of the Youth Ministry Department at Trinity College in Deerfield, Illinois. He has over 10 years' experience in youth ministry, and is a popular retreat and conference speaker as well as a Youth Ministry Consultant for Lay Renewal Ministries of St. Louis, Missouri. Small group ministry is a primary focus as he disciples students and equips them for leadership.

All Bible quotations, unless otherwise indicated, are from the *Holy Bible, New International Version,* © 1973, 1978, 1984, International Bible Society. Used by permission of Zondervan Bible Publishers.

ISBN: 0-89693-042-4

1 2 3 4 5 6 7 8 9 10 Printing/Year 94 93 92 91 90

© 1990, SP Publications, Inc. All rights reserved.
Printed in the United States of America.

CONTENTS

Introduction   5

1 Putting Your Emotions on ICE   9
A practical strategy for responding to emotions without freezing them out

2 I've Lost That Loving Feeling   22
Jesus demonstrates that love is a commitment, not just a feeling

3 I Love Me, I Love Me Not   32
Giving and receiving affirmation of who we are in Christ

4 Hope Is on the Way!   41
Overcoming feelings of despair

5 I'm Getting Very Angry   52
Learning to apply the biblical pattern of resolution

6 Crowd Control   63
Making smart decisions despite emotional pressures

INTRODUCTION

Small Group Studies

Small group studies are designed to create an environment for your group members which will (1) provide acceptance for them just as they are, (2) challenge them with God's truth to be who He calls them to be, and (3) offer a supportive community to strengthen their personal and spiritual growth. Within the context of meaningful, interpersonal relationships, each session seeks the healing and wholeness of persons through their personal encounters with the grace and holiness of Jesus Christ. Just as the community grew together in Acts 2, as the body served together in 1 Corinthians 12, and the church was equipped together in Ephesians 4, so will your group experience the reality that in Christ we become more than just the sum of our individual members when we meet together, just as we are, to become just who He calls us to be.

Contemporary culture, specifically that of adolescents, offers very little opportunity for interpersonal intimacy. Students need a safe place for healing and a supportive place for growth into wholeness. They need a place to go where they can take off the masks they use to cover insecurity and uncertainty about who they are as persons. They are also searching for a place where they can find meaning through making a contribution to the lives of others. Your students require the security of belonging to a significant community of peers in order to develop their own identity in Christ. Small group studies enable you to meet these needs for individuals who are at all levels of personal and spiritual maturity. The only prerequisite for being a member of these small groups is a heart willing to develop relationships with friends. The potential for growth is as limitless as the potential for God's work in your individual and corporate lives.

To introduce you to the process of small group studies, an overview of the format has been provided.

SESSION OVERVIEW
Each session begins with a summary of the small group experience which has been prepared for your group.

Purpose states the intent of the session, clearly defining the overall thrust of this particular small group experience.

Needs briefly examines the needs of group members in relation to the topic and Scripture. Attention will also be given to issues in light of the interpersonal structure of each session.

Goals list objectives by which you can (1) adapt the materials specifically for the context of the small group with which you are working and (2) evaluate the effectiveness of the session in measurable terms.

Life Response suggests a commitment each group member can make in living out the lesson during the week. Additional suggestions for groups with higher commitment levels follow each session.

Resource Materials outlines what you will need in order

INTRODUCTION

to lead the group through each session.

♥ HEARTBEAT

These opening exercises and experiences are designed to take a pulse, to get to the heart of who students are. They focus group members on the question, "Who am I?" Active listening and accurate affirmation are the key ingredients in this first step toward community building.

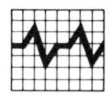

⩘ LIFELINE

Discovery is the dynamic element in these active studies of God's Word. The personal, practical exploration of "who I am called to be" is the focus of the group's interaction with biblical truth. As group members deepen in their knowledge and broaden in their understanding of Jesus Christ's lordship, they will be directed toward relevant application of this truth in their own personal context.

✶ BODYLIFE

Your group members will experience the reality of the love of the Body as they commit themselves corporately to being all of who God calls them to be. Personal ownership of the truth discovered in LIFELINE enables students to make new commitments toward personal and spiritual growth. Through affirmation, prayer, and encouragement, they will realize that the love in Christian peer support is greater than the fear of the world's peer pressure.

HINTS & HELPS

☞ **HELPS:** are provided to sensitize you to student concerns and questions which may arise in response to the topic or structure of the session. These insights and resources will help you prepare for the challenges of leading a small group through the community experience of being who God calls them to be.

☞ **HINTS:** are provided to develop your own small group leadership skills. These technical points of advice will support you in your challenging role.

GROUP MEMBER AND LEADER MATERIALS
Group members' workbooks include the main content of the HEARTBEAT, LIFELINE, and BODYLIFE sections of each session. All of the group members' material is reproduced in your leader's edition. Additional exercises and activities in the leader's edition are printed in **boldface**. These additional resources are designed to allow you maximum flexibility for working with your group.

PREPARATION
Your preparation as leader will consist mainly of becoming familiar with the purposes, needs, and goals of each session and adapting the session content in light of your own group. Some groups will need to begin the series with an added emphasis upon the HEARTBEAT section. Other groups, either because of group members' personal maturity or depth of relationships, will have a community foundation which will enable them to focus more time in the LIFELINE and BODYLIFE sections. In either case, you will be prepared to meet students at their points of need.

Group members will not need to prepare in advance for the sessions. As the LIFELINE and BODYLIFE sections become more of a reality, however, student commitments will establish the need for follow-through and loving, community accountability. This accountability can be very naturally incorporated into the following session's HEARTBEAT section once students have progressed to this point.

Prayer will be the ultimate source of preparation for both you and your group. The materials provided for you will encourage and support your efforts to integrate prayer into every phase of this small group series.

ONE
▼
Putting Your Emotions on ICE

SESSION OVERVIEW

Purpose:
"Putting Your Emotions on ICE," the first group meeting in *Can't Fight the Feelings,* leads the participants to examine the issues related to making choices in response to their changing emotions. Group members will discover that, while they cannot choose how they feel, they can choose how they will deal with those feelings. Group members should come to an understanding of emotions as both neutral and natural. Their personal choices determine whether or not their emotions become negative or positive influences.

Needs:
Adolescents are vulnerable to a variety of changing emotions. Their emotions are very intense and at times seem overwhelming to them. They may say or do certain things simply because they are feeling strong emotions which they do not know how to control. Your group members need to understand that, although they may not always be able to determine their emotions, they can control the influ-

ence of those feelings. This self-control begins with learning to work through emotions as a preparation for making good decisions.

Goals:
The goals for the *leader* include
(1) creating an atmosphere in which group members can discuss their feelings openly and without fear of rejection or ridicule;
(2) guiding group members to an acceptance of their feelings as neutral and natural;
(3) beginning to equip group members with the resources they will need to make biblical decisions in the midst of changing emotions.

The goals for the *group members* are that they will
(1) view their emotions as acceptable to God;
(2) practice the ICE (Identify-Clarify-Exemplify) pattern for dealing with emotions;
(3) begin to take responsibility for not being controlled by their emotions;
(4) perceive this small group as a place where their concerns and feelings will be responded to positively;
(5) commit themselves to supporting one another in this process of becoming truth-controlled rather than emotion-controlled.

Life Response:
Based upon their understanding of the process of Identify-Clarify-Exemplify, the group members will verbally commit to accepting and encouraging one another in this process during the next five group sharing times.

Resource Materials:
___ Bibles
___ slips of paper with the sentences for the first activity
___ one copy of *Can't Fight the Feelings* for each member

PUTTING YOUR EMOTIONS ON ICE

♡ HEARTBEAT

To create an atmosphere in which group members learn to share with one another, use the discussion activity outlined below. It will provide a non-threatening way for students to talk about themselves.

☞ [HINT: Always begin small group times sitting comfortably in a circle so that all members of the group can make eye contact. Affirm each answer or comment made. These two elements are essential as you seek to facilitate community and bond-building within the group.]

In bowl —

Write the following incomplete statements on slips of paper prior to the group meeting:
1. Most weekends I feel like I want to. . . .
2. The teacher I have liked most was. . . .
3. One thing I would like to do in my life is. . . .
4. One thing which I really enjoy doing is. . . .
5. A movie that I thought was great was. . . .
6. A friend who is important to me is. . . .
7. A time in my life when I was happy was. . . .
8. The perfect day for me would be. . . .
9. The qualities I most want in my friends are. . . .
10. Someone who cares about me is. . . .

Fold the 10 slips of paper and place them in a bag or a bowl. Pass the container of slips to the first person in the circle. Taking turns, each person will draw one slip out of the container, read it and then put it back so that it may be drawn again. That person will then complete the statement as it applies to his or her own life.

In the first round, simply have each person respond without any additional questions or discussion taking place among the group.

Begin round two with the instructions that the

11

CAN'T FIGHT THE FEELINGS

group is now allowed to ask questions of the person after he or she completes the statement. Or, as a variation, ask each person to automatically explain his or her answer. This second round will produce interaction among the group members as well as lead them to speak more personally about themselves.

If your group members don't know one another, have them preface each answer with some piece of personal data, such as name, age, school, hobbies or interests, etc.

It has been said, "If you can't beat 'em, then join 'em." If only it were that simple when it comes to dealing with our emotions.

Have you ever wished your emotions would just go away because you were tired of feeling hurt? Feelings like sadness or bitterness are emotions that no one wants to have to live with. On the other hand, there are some feelings you want to last forever. If you have ever "fallen in love" you probably hoped that those feelings would never leave you!

Because we cannot simply turn our emotions on and off whenever we want, we must learn how to deal with the great mix of feelings that is a part of our lives. For the next six weeks we will talk about our emotions and learn more about what we can do when all those feelings seem so strong that we begin to feel out of control.

Feelings . . .

Let's start with a list of all the emotions that we can imagine ourselves experiencing.

☞ [HINT: Brainstorming is a method of discovery learning in which participants call out all that they can think of in response to a question. This is done without the leader or the group taking time to evaluate the responses.

PUTTING YOUR EMOTIONS ON ICE

Invite group members to call out any ideas they have, then list them, and take time to discuss and evaluate them only after you have completed the brainstorming activity.]

Now place a check by any of these emotions which you have felt this past week.

☞ [HINT: Having individuals write their responses ensures that they will have something to share with the group. It does not mean, however, that they will want to share with everyone else.

As the facilitator of discussion, reinforce to the group members that there is no right or wrong answer in this type of question. Rather, this is a chance for all of you to talk about both your unique and your common experiences in preparation for better understanding how you can be supportive of each other as you grow together.

You can communicate this by giving positive affirmation to each response, encouraging group members to listen for things they may have in common with each other as well as things they can learn from each other, and asking them to share only to the degree that they feel comfortable.]

Now circle the emotions that seem to be "bad" and underline the ones that seem to be "good."

☞ [HELP: When students are choosing "good" and "bad" emotions, emphasize that it is to be the emotions which *seem* good or bad. It is important that they do not conclude too early whether there are such things as good or bad feelings. The important thing at this point is to acknowledge that some emotions are considered undesirable and others are considered attractive.]

13

CAN'T FIGHT THE FEELINGS

In a few minutes we will answer these questions:
1. Is it sinful to have "bad" emotions?
2. Can emotions really be called "bad"?

☞ **[HELP: This first section is to set up the discovery which will take place in the LIFELINE section. It is not important that group members know correct answers at this point.]**

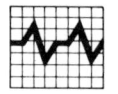

LIFELINE

Let's look at some of the emotions of Jesus found in the following passages: Matthew 21:12-13; Matthew 23:12-36; Matthew 26:37-46; Matthew 27:46; Luke 19:41; John 11:35.

☞ **[HINT: If your group is actively and openly discussing at this point, you may want to go through this section in a large group dialogue. If they seem hesitant to share, divide them into smaller groups and have them work together, writing out their answers to the questions in preparation for a large group discussion.]**

List what Jesus seemed to be feeling in these moments of His life and what was happening that brought out these feelings.

Did any of these emotions make our "bad" list in the HEARTBEAT section?

Based on these verses, is it sinful to have "bad" emotions? Explain.

☞ **[HELP: Dealing with Jesus' human attributes is not always an easy process. Certain emotions may be associated with weakness or even sin in the student's experience. Be sure to allow group members to discover what is found in each text and discuss fully that since** both the humanity and the divinity of Jesus imply emotions (God Himself is attributed with feelings as a personal God), we can be confident that emotions are neither sinful or weak in themselves.]

Should difficult or painful emotions really be labeled as "bad"? Explain.

☞ [HELP: Undesirable does not mean bad. A person who is hurt or angry is not necessarily guilty, though he may wish those feelings would leave. Sin enters not in the feelings but in the willing.]

Feeling & Willing
When we experience emotions which are not fun or feel bad, we have several choices about what to do with those emotions. Following are three examples of how people chose to deal with the painful feelings brought about by their belief that no one really cared about who they were on the inside.

☞ [HINT: Invite three group members to read these aloud for the group. In this way students continue to actively participate and you continue to be more of a facilitator than the instructor who gives all the answers.]

Stuffed Stuart just kept all of his hurt and anger inside. He never talked about why he thought no one loved him, and he always just assumed he was right. He kept his feelings so bottled up that he sometimes thought he was going to explode. He even got to the point that he was afraid to show any emotion for fear that all these stuffed emotions would go off like gunpowder. Happy or sad, excited or depressed, Stuart just stuffed it all inside himself.

Denial Daniel pretended everything was great. He did not want anyone to know that he was hurting and lonely. He was always funny and creative with his friends. "The Life of the Party" was his label. Sometimes when he was alone, however, the thought that no one understood or loved the real Daniel would flood his mind. Soon the feelings of hurt and depression would start to surface. When this happened he just got busy working or called up a friend or watched television so the thoughts and the pain would go away. Because he denied his painful emotions, if someone asked Daniel how he was feeling, he always said, "Life is great!"

Dangerous Dora was like a volcano around her friends. They never knew when she would erupt with yelling or critical comments toward the people around her. No one escaped her outbursts—not teachers, parents, or friends. She had the idea that if someone hurt her feelings then it was their problem if she hurt them back. After she did hurt someone else, however, she often began to feel guilty and would later apologize to the person for the way she had treated him.

☞ [HINT: Have group members work in twos or threes to answer the following questions, giving them a chance to learn from each other.]

What are some current or potential problems you can observe in the ways Stuart, Daniel, and Dora are dealing with their emotions?

What would you say to them if they were your friends?

You Make the Call!
All of us experience what we listed above as "good" and "bad" emotions. In reality, because these emotions are not sinful, they are not necessarily bad or good. Emotions themselves are neutral. And having emotions that feel good or emotions that feel bad is only natural.

PUTTING YOUR EMOTIONS ON ICE

☞ **[HINT: Again, let group members do the reading here. You may wish to ask, "What do you think about this?" or "Have you found this to be true in your experience?" in order to get students to interact with the material.]**

The important issue facing us when we feel a certain way is, "What will we choose to do with those feelings?" Dealing with emotions involves making decisions. To choose to stuff feelings inside, ignore them, or take them out on others can seriously hurt us in our relationships with God, family, and friends.

ICE It!

Here is a pattern we can use to understand, explore, and evaluate our emotions so that we can make decisions that are not just based on how we feel.

Identify the feelings. What is it exactly that you are feeling? Would you describe yourself as angry, happy, sad, scared? Accept these emotions as neutral and natural.

Clarify the source. What is happening in your life or what are you thinking that results in your feeling this way? Realize that there is usually a change in your circumstances or your relationships or your thinking that is at the root of your emotional responses.

☞ **[HELP: This is not always true. Sometimes, especially with adolescents, feelings change due to the stresses of simply maturing and developing. Be sure to acknowledge to your group the validity of times when they really do not know why they feel the way they do. In those times, the process of clarifying the source remains important because it helps them recognize the emotion for what it is, a reaction that will eventually pass.]**

Exemplify Christ in your choices. What is the best way for you to respond to your circumstances, relationships, or stress or to adjust your thinking so that you can glorify Christ in this situation? Trust that you can learn to make choices based on the truth, not just on what you feel.

BODYLIFE

☞ [HINT: The purpose of this summary quiz is to review what has been discovered in preparation for application of this new insight.]

Choose one:
    Emotions are all good.
    Emotions are all bad.
    Some emotions are good; others are bad.
    Emotions themselves are not good or bad; it is the choices we make which are good and bad.

Stuart stuffs, Daniel just denies, and Dora explodes at random when feeling strong emotions. Share with the group times when you have seen friends or others who seem to follow the example of Stuart, Daniel, or Dora.

☞ [HELP: Specific questions which will stimulate this sharing include:
- What are some other ways in which your parents deal with their emotions? How do your peers deal with emotions?
- When you experience strong emotions, how are you most likely to deal with them?

Notice the progression of the questions. We begin with a question about fictional persons. Next the group members respond from their observations of their parents, then their peers. Finally, they reply as to themselves. Group members are thus progressively brought into more personal self-disclosure. Moving from what

they think about others to themselves allows them the opportunity to gain the confidence to be more honest.]

Complete the words. A good pattern to follow is:
I
C
E

What would be different if Stuart, Daniel, or Dora were to use the pattern of "putting their emotions on ICE" in dealing with their emotions?

☞ [HELP: Encourage group members to discuss how this would have affected each of these persons individually as well as how it would have helped them in their relationships with others.]

Life Response

We are going to make our group times together work with a commitment to one another to do the following:

1. Listen to one another as we identify how we feel;

2. Accept one another's feelings as natural and neutral;

3. Discuss together what is happening in our lives that seems to be the source of our emotional responses;

4. Encourage one another to exemplify Christ by doing what is right in our relationships with God, family, and friends as we grow together in this group.

☞ [HINT: When making this type of commitment, be certain that all the group members are actively involved. We don't want to just ask them if they will do this so that their investment in the initial commitment is merely to say yes. We want them to meaningfully affirm this commitment before God and one another.

This can be done by having them write a prayer to God or pray out loud to God concerning this commitment or to have them sign their names under a commitment which has been written out by the group. In this way they are witnesses together of the importance of the commitment they are making and their serious intention to keep it.]

☞ [HELP: In addition to the LIFE RESPONSE, your group may be ready for some follow-through activities. These additional optional LIFE RESPONSES are ways in which your group can practically apply this content in preparation for their next group sharing time.

1. Group members can keep an ICE journal of their feelings this week. In the journal they can log their specific feelings, describe what they think are the sources of those feelings, and write the choices they have, including the one they think would most exemplify Christ.

2. Group members could observe other people at home, school, and church to determine how they seem to deal with their emotions. They can take note of the results they see from these different patterns of responses to emotions.

3. During their personal devotional times, group members may want to read the passages for the next group sharing time. Ask them to consider what feelings they would associate with the word "love." In this way they will be prepared to contribute more deeply and personally as they begin the next group time.

All of the follow-through options in this series may be given as mere suggestions or as actual assignments members are asked to commit to as a part of the group. Your approach will depend on the maturity and commitment level of the group. If you do have students making serious commitments to do LIFE RESPONSES, be certain that you include follow-up in the

PUTTING YOUR EMOTIONS ON ICE

subsequent group experience. As a leader, you model the importance of their commitments, as well as how to deal with failure in meeting those expectations, by the way you work through the follow-up of their accountability.]

What's Next?

"I've Lost That Loving Feeling" — How can you have a love that lasts when the feelings are gone?

TWO

▼

I've Lost That Loving Feeling

SESSION OVERVIEW

Purpose:
In "I've Lost That Loving Feeling" group members will learn that true love is a commitment that is not determined by one's emotions. Having discovered the commitment of Jesus' true love for them, group members will explore practical ways in which they can learn to love with a love that is greater than their emotions.

Needs:
Adolescents are captivated by feelings of love. They fall in and out of love on almost a regular basis. One day that certain guy or girl is the greatest person in the world; the next day they do not even want to be in the same world as that formerly wonderful person.

Your group members want true love, but often confuse their romantic infatuations with true love because of the intensity of these emotions. This is to be expected and accepted.

You can, however, help group members begin to look beyond their desired emotions of "being in love" to understand that true love does not change with feelings. The love of Jesus and that love expressed in friendship with others is available to them whether they have a boyfriend or girlfriend or not. It is a love which is willing to suffer and be hurt as well as rejoice. Group members need to understand that this true love is most important in their lives and most important for them to learn to share.

Goals:
The goals for the *leader* include
(1) leading the group through a discovery of the emotions which are associated with love;
(2) supporting group members with affirmation and acceptance as they role-play life situations;
(3) serving not as their commander but as their coach as they practice applying their new pattern to love relationships.

The goals for the *group members* are that they
(1) challenge themselves to love with Jesus' love;
(2) learn to evaluate true love by its commitment rather than by its emotions;
(3) commit to learning together what it means to experience true love on a deeper level, regardless of where each of them may be at this point.

Life Response:
Group members will write a set of "Love Laws" which will serve as their standard of commitment to one another. These guidelines, rather than their feelings, are to be the group's bases for behaving in love.

Resource Materials:
___ Bibles
___ stopwatch or watch with a second hand
___ scrap paper
___ one copy of *Can't Fight the Feelings* for each member

❤ HEARTBEAT

☞ [HINT: Just a reminder: in a circle, comfortably seated for good eye contact.]

Learning to identify, clarify, and exemplify involves working through some very desirable feelings as well as some very painful ones. Let's begin this group time by exploring a feeling each of us wants to receive and give: love.

To start our discussion we will divide into two teams for a debate. The topic will be: RESOLVED: LOVE IS JUST A FEELING.

The affirmative side will argue for two minutes that love is primarily an emotion which changes. This side will support the concept of being committed but contend that those commitments will change according to feelings.

The negative side will respond with its own two-minute argument that love is not an emotion as much as it is a commitment. Love involves emotions, but it does not change its constant commitment.

Following these opening arguments, each side will be given three minutes to prepare a one-minute rebuttal.

> Give each side 8–10 minutes to prepare a 2-minute argument. You will judge the debate based on their arguments. Encourage them to use examples and persuasive points. Remind them that the issue is not whether they agree or disagree with their side, the point is to prepare the best possible argument.
> After the debate it will be important to let individuals voice their own opinions about this subject. Take note of two cautions:

I'VE LOST THAT LOVING FEELING

First, prepare the students not to take any of their arguments personally or to use personal attacks as a part of the debate. This discussion, as with any good debate, is about the issue only.

Second, maintain the tension between the two sides. If they pick up from you that theirs is a right answer, then one side will feel defeated before it begins. The point of having this debate is to raise the tension between love as a commitment and love as a feeling so that the truth can be discovered.

☞ [HINT: Debates with younger adolescents may require adult leadership to organize and focus their ideas. Keep the maturity factor of your group in mind when you use this method.]

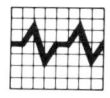

LIFELINE

☞ [HINT: If the discussion is lively and group members are open, you can keep the entire group together through this LIFELINE section. If not, you may want to assign smaller groups to work together so that each member takes an active part.]

Read John 13:1-11. What feelings might Jesus have been experiencing as He washed the disciples' feet? Peter's feet? Judas' feet? Describe how these disciples may have been feeling.

☞ [HINT: Prompt hesitant group members by asking them, "How would you have felt if you were Peter, Judas, the others?"]

Read Mark 15:22-41 and Luke 23:33-49. What feelings might Jesus have been experiencing during these final hours? Was it an act of love for Jesus to experience this pain and suffering? Explain.

CAN'T FIGHT THE FEELINGS

☞ **[HELP: Group members can begin to see that Jesus was not feeling "warm fuzzies" when He was fulfilling His greatest act of love.** In a culture where love is often defined as "getting," your group members need to discover that Jesus' love was one of giving. He did not ask, "What's in it for me?" nor did He rely on His emotional needs as the basis of His love. This is evidenced by the emotional torment and agony he was obviously experiencing.]

In what ways do you think Jesus' love in these two instances was a mixture of desirable feelings as well as painful ones? What do we learn about Jesus' love from these verses?

☞ **[HELP: The love Jesus offers is well acquainted with sorrows and rejection. Jesus is the ultimate example of love that does not change with circumstances or feelings.]**

Read John 13:34-35. If our love is to be like that of Jesus, what type of emotions might we expect to experience?

Read 1 Corinthians 13:4-8. List all the qualities of love found in these verses.

These verses portray love as an action, a commitment to another person. When you are feeling loving toward someone, action and commitment are easy. They are not so easy when you get into an argument or someone has selfishly hurt you. Circle the action in the list that is the hardest for you to do when you are not feeling love toward the person you are trying to love.

☞ **[HELP: Most people understand that love should be something that goes beyond feelings. Many of your group members have experienced relationships which

I'VE LOST THAT LOVING FEELING

reflect commitment, such as those with parents or close friends. These relationships can serve as an excellent beginning point for understanding how to act in love when they do not feel like loving. Recognize, however, that some group members may be skeptical or even cynical about the reality of love as a true commitment if they have experienced the brokenness of divorce or have always felt distant from their family members.]

Who is a person in your life that you would choose to act in love toward even if you were not feeling any love for him or her at the time? Why would you do this? What does that tell you about your love for that person? In what ways is this like the love of Jesus?

BODYLIFE

Take this group quiz to review what we've talked about so far.

☞ [HINT: Work together as a group to summarize the review material in preparation for specific application in this session.]

1. Biblical love like that of Jesus and that described by Paul in 1 Corinthians is primarily a feeling. TRUE / FALSE

2. Working together, let's fill in the blank: LOVE IS. . . .

☞ [HELP: Any definition should include the concept of commitment.]

3. Whether we feel loving toward a person or unloving, we can seek to act in love by putting those emotions on ICE. ICE stands for: I _____, C _____, E _____.

☞ [HELP: Group members need to understand that just as not feeling love does not mean that we cannot act in love toward someone, feeling love does not mean that we automatically are committed to loving that person.

Sometimes we need to ICE loving feelings to avoid promising more than we can give in a relationship, only to discover that we are not really committed and then abandoning the relationship.]

Have one of the members read the following case study aloud for the group.

Case Study

Jill and Carolyn have been best friends ever since they met as members of the school band their freshman year at Taylor High School. Now that they are seniors, both are trying to decide what they will do when they graduate.

Both have applied for admission to Galesborough College, an exclusive school on the East Coast. Recently Jill found out that she was accepted, but Carolyn discovered that she would have to raise her test scores in order to get in. Carolyn thinks Jill is so excited about going to Galesborough that she does not even care that she may not be able to go with her. It seems to Carolyn that all Jill ever talks about is "next year at Galesborough." Carolyn always thought that if Jill did not get accepted that she would not go either. Now she cannot believe that Jill does not even seem concerned about leaving her behind.

> Invite members of the group to take turns role-playing as a friend of Carolyn and Jill. You as the leader will play Carolyn. Encourage role-players to talk with Carolyn as if she were a member of your small group who was trying to apply the Identify-Clarify-Exemplify principles to this situation.
> The role play begins with Carolyn saying, "I just

can't stand Jill!" The first participant will begin by responding to Carolyn [you].

☞ [HINT: It is not important whether guys play Carolyn or her friends. You are literally playing a role and that does not depend on your own gender.

Announce ahead of time to the group that each person will talk for only a few moments, and then someone else will pick up right where the last person ended. This gets everyone involved and listening and keeps any one person from being under too much pressure.

Let role plays move quickly, and stop whenever group members are dealing with the issues you want them to experience. After role plays, be sure to use debriefing questions like the following, which will help participants talk about the experience and evaluate their responses.]

Questions for this role play can include:
- What were some of the feelings Carolyn was experiencing?
- What seemed to be causing these feelings?
- What was hard about this for you as her friend?
- What are your concerns for Carolyn and Jill as they work through their friendship?
- What options does Carolyn have at this point?
- How could Carolyn act out of love for Jill in this situation?
- How could Jill respond in love?

☞ [HINT: After a good discussion and evaluation of the role play experience, it is sometimes helpful, though not always, to replay the role play using this new insight and information to see how it increases the effectiveness of the skill you are trying to develop.]

Share a specific example of someone in your life at this

time that you want to love, though you do not always feel loving toward that person.

Whether love begins or grows with emotions, it takes the will to make it work. List some ways this group can specifically grow in its actions of love toward one another.

☞ [HELP: In other words, how can they specifically apply what they have learned from the Bible study and the role play to the way they are to act in love toward one another?]

Life Response

As a group, let's write a set of "Love Laws" or guidelines stating the principles we have learned. These guidelines represent our commitment to exemplify Christ through true love for one another even when we've "lost that loving feeling."

☞ **[HELP: Possible "Love Laws" could include:**
- **We will choose to work at being supportive when others are hurting.**
- **We will choose to forgive one another because Christ has forgiven us.**
- **We will not demand service from others in order to earn our love.**
- **We will not let anger turn into bitterness by harboring resentment toward one another; we will forgive and *forget*.**
- **We will listen to one another's thoughts and feelings because they are important.**
- **We will look for ways to serve each other's needs rather than waiting for them to ask.**
- **We will look for the good in each other, to affirm and appreciate.**

This set of standards illustrates that love is a commitment. Love is not just saying these standards or writing them. True love is the doing of love. As a group you will be able to refer to these as you grow together and as you learn to effectively support one another in your reaching out to love those outside the group.]

☞ [HELP: Optional additional LIFE RESPONSES for follow-through:
    1. Group members may want to write out specific ways in which they will choose to act in love toward someone with whom they are currently experiencing a conflict. They can use the ICE pattern this next week to enable them to keep this commitment. Asking the others in the group to prayerfully support them and hold them accountable next week would be a great bond-building experience for the group as well.
    2. Group members could make copies of the "Love Laws" and place them in their Bibles or on a wall at home as a reminder to pray for one another. This could also serve as a stimulus for thinking of specific ways to share love with one another through writing, personal encouragement, prayer, or serving one another by meeting a need such as helping with a project at home or school.]

What's Next?

"I Love Me, I Love Me Not" — How do you keep loving others when you don't feel like loving yourself?

THREE

I Love Me, I Love Me Not

SESSION OVERVIEW

Purpose:
In "I Love Me, I Love Me Not," group members will recognize that the truth of Scripture is the basis of their self-esteem and that they can help each other experience the self-worth we have in Christ by committing themselves to affirming one another.

Needs:
Adolescents are in the period of life when they first become able to place themselves in another's perspective. Someone has said that adolescents reason about themselves in this way: "I am not who I think I am, I am not who you think I am, I am who I think you think I am."

Many of your group members look to others to mirror who they are. They perceive themselves as not measuring up because they think that others see their inferiorities. They often feel ugly and odd, and they can be very self-conscious. They need truth that goes beyond their feelings about themselves. They need objective facts to fall back on as the basis for their self-worth.

Goals:

The *leader's* goals include
(1) affirming group members as they discuss their feelings about themselves;
(2) enabling group members to discover how God views them;
(3) facilitating significant peer affirmation among group members.

The goals for *group members* are that they
(1) acknowledge the struggles they face in loving themselves;
(2) write a biblically based declarative statement about their self-worth;
(3) express and receive affirmation of one another's worth in Christ.

Life Response:

The group members will (1) write a declarative statement about their own self-worth in Christ; (2) model God's perspective of one another in a time of personal affirmation.

Resource Materials:
___ Bibles
___ ball of yarn or thick string
___ one copy of *Can't Fight the Feelings* for each member

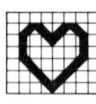

♥ HEARTBEAT

> [HINT: As you work through these sessions, if group members are committing to LIFE RESPONSES, it will be important for you to incorporate a time of sharing together concerning the results of those commitments. This can be done in the early stages of the group meeting or in more informal discussions either before or after the meeting. The key point is that group members need your help in processing their feelings and thoughts about their life responses.]

Loving someone is a choice of the heart that involves more than just feelings. As we read last week in 1 Corinthians 13, real love is an action based on commitment.

> [HINT: You may want to take a moment to review for those who were absent.]

This applies not only to the love that we are to have for our family and friends but to our love for ourselves as well. To begin to understand more about the commitment to love ourselves, let's begin by sharing some feelings about ourselves.

> [HINT: Discuss the first three statements before continuing. This will enable the group to build trust and acceptance in preparation for the more personally revealing questions which follow.]

1. Qualities about myself which I like are. . . .

2. Qualities about myself I would like to change are. . . .

3. Qualities which others like most about me are. . . .

4. The feelings which I most often have about myself are (choose two): anger, disappointment, joy, thankfulness, guilt, uncertainty, contentment, peacefulness, anxiety, pride, other: _____.

5. I have thought the following about myself at one time or another:
   a. "I am a loser."
   b. "I am a failure."
   c. "I am important."
   d. "I am stupid."
   e. "I am a good person."
   f. "I am no good to anybody."
   g. "I am different than my friends."
   h. "I am unlovable."
   i. "I am _____."

6. One time when I felt especially positive or negative about myself was when I. . . .

☞ **[HINT: These thoughts and feelings may be difficult for some members to discuss with the group. Model vulnerability by being honest about your own experiences, both positive and negative. You can help group members see that everyone suffers through feelings of inferiority at times.]**

Painful feelings about ourselves may lead us to see ourselves as ugly, unimportant, or unlovable. Positive feelings may lead us to see ourselves as valuable and lovable. These feelings will change back and forth. What is the truth? Are you lovable? If so, how can you learn to act in love toward yourself even when you don't feel like it?

A number of things lead us to develop negative feelings about ourselves. Sometimes things happen in our lives that we blame ourselves for causing or not preventing. For instance, our parents divorce or we are left out of the group at school to which we want to belong. We think we are to blame for not being good enough or attractive enough or "whatever enough" to be loved as we want to be. Or maybe we compare ourselves to a brother or sister who seems more talented or to friends who seem more successful. We can even compare ourselves to our own idea of who God wants us to be. We may begin to feel that God's love, like our feelings about ourselves, changes. We may feel that He loves us when we are good, but does not love us when we are bad.

☞ **[HINT: To understand more of what group members have observed or experienced, ask them for specific examples of what causes them to feel bad about themselves.]**

Since we all experience these feelings, it is important that we try to find out the truth about God's love for us and how it affects our love for ourselves.

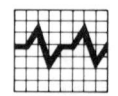

LIFELINE

As strange as it may seem, we begin to love ourselves with God's love when we acknowledge that we are not good enough! We have all sinned and we do not measure up to God's righteous standards.

Then how can I love myself? If I am not good enough how can I be worthy of God's love—or any other love, for that matter?

The answer is: GRACE.

The Grace to Be Not Good Enough
Read Ephesians 2:8-9. Rewrite these verses in your own words explaining what they mean.

If you are a Christian, then you are saved by grace. Because you are saved by grace, two things are absolutely FALSE, no matter how you feel:

1. You are condemned and unlovable to God because of your sins.

2. You are a loser compared to others.

THEREFORE, two things are absolutely TRUE:

True Statement One
You are not condemned and you are lovable to God because of Jesus Christ in you.

In pairs, read Romans 8:1-2. Then briefly answer these questions:

• What do you think of when you think of the word "condemnation"?

• What does Paul seem to mean by stating that there is no condemnation in Christ Jesus?

• What do you think is the difference between being convicted and condemned?

☞ **[HELP: Your group members need to understand that, while God still works through His Word and Spirit to *convict* them of sin, because of Jesus' atonement God no longer *condemns* them. Jesus truly forgives those who repent, and the love of Jesus allows all believers to enjoy fully the love of the Father. We Christians must be willing to grow as God convicts us of sin, but we should never subject ourselves to thoughts of condemnation, because Christ has set us free from the laws of sin and death.]**

True Statement Two
You are unique and valuable to God because of Jesus Christ in you.

In pairs again, reread Ephesians 2:8-9 and read verse 10 as well.

- What has God prepared for you in Christ?

- What is the basis for seeing yourself as unique and valuable according to these verses?

- How could seeing yourself as saved by grace and created as His workmanship keep you from comparing yourself to others?

☞ **[HELP: Grace removes the need for comparison because our goodness is found in being who God created us to be, not in being "better" than someone else.]**

Two TRUTHS which I can state about myself in Christ are that. . . .

☞ **[HELP: Group members can learn that (1) each Christian can enjoy God's unconditional love forever and (2) each Christian can be free from comparison because God works uniquely in each of our lives.]**

BODYLIFE
If we never have to worry about losing God's love as Christians and if we do not have to live by comparisons, then how does that affect the ways we treat each other?

☞ **[HELP: Discuss how to model love for one another by choosing to encourage and enable rather than to compete and compare.]**

Life Response

Summarize this discussion by writing out a declarative statement of how you can be supportive of one another's growth in self-worth. Begin this statement with, "When one of our Christian friends feels condemned or not good enough...."

☞ [HELP: An example of a declarative statement: When one of our Christian friends feels condemned or not good enough, we can support that person by helping him or her say, "I am who I am by the grace of God." This begins by my accepting that person for who he or she is.]

The "grace bomb" is a way for group members to practice mirroring God's love for who they are. Begin with a ball of yarn or string in your hand and explain the experience as follows.

"This 'grace bomb' is an opportunity for you to share with one another the way you see each other as lovable and unique. I will begin by sharing with the group something which I appreciate and love about another person in the circle without naming that person. When I have finished, I will toss the yarn to that person. That person will then repeat the process, sharing about someone else." The result will be a string of yarn connecting all of you to show the grace God has given you to be one in Him.

☞ [HELP: Communicate to the group that affirmation is not about external appearance or performance (i.e., you are a beautiful girl or you are a great athlete) but rather one of recognizing attributes (i.e., you are sensitive or you are always sincere).]

Close in prayer thanking God specifically for each individual.

☞ [HELP: Additional optional LIFE RESPONSES:
1. Group members may want to take time to list all of the affirming statements that were made about them in this small group. They can keep them on a mirror or in a school notebook to remind them that they are special in Christ even when they feel inferior by comparison to others.
2. The two positive declarations made from Scripture would be great for your group members to memorize along with the Scriptures themselves (Ephesians 2:8-10, Romans 8:1-2). When they experience self-doubt or feelings of condemnation they could refer to these truths as the basis for loving themselves as Christ has loved them.
3. Group members may want to keep a log where they ICE their feelings about themselves between now and next week. They could then share the way God is teaching them to exemplify Christ's love for themselves.

What's Next?

"Hope is on the Way!" — What can you hope for when you are feeling hopeless?

FOUR

▼

Hope Is on the Way!

SESSION OVERVIEW

Purpose:
In this group experience, "Hope Is on the Way!" group members will be challenged to develop an understanding of biblical truth that will lead them to turn to God in times of despair. They will work through the source of feelings of despair and find confidence in the One who is greater than the feelings and the circumstances surrounding those feelings.

Needs:
Adolescents battle with feelings of worthlessness, hopelessness, and helplessness as a part of their developmental process. Not quite adults but no longer children, they often feel lost in between. They view themselves as isolated and uncertain because of the insecurity and instability they are facing in this time of transition. Their growing bodies and expanding mental capacities drain them of emotional energy. Add to this mixture a broken relationship at school or a divorce at home or a failure to achieve a goal, and despair can quickly set in.

CAN'T FIGHT THE FEELINGS

In response to these feelings and their potential harm, your group members need to learn how to acknowledge their feelings of worthlessness, helplessness, and hopelessness without being ashamed or feeling guilty. This is the beginning point, but group members must be equipped to go beyond mere awareness to actively choosing to find worth, help, and hope in God. He provides the basis for dealing with despair so that it is not turned inward to harm themselves or outward to hurt others.

Goals:
The goals for the *leader* include
(1) listening for levels of despair which might indicate suicidal thoughts;
(2) enabling group members to realize that everyone feels some degree of despair at times;
(3) creating an atmosphere where it is not considered weak or sinful to have these feelings;
(4) leading group members to discover that they can choose to seek God and trust Him to be their rescuer from despair.

The goals for *group members* are that they
(1) identify their own struggles with despair;
(2) understand the three emotional roots of despair;
(3) seek God's truth as the answer to despair;
(4) experience how they can support others.

Life Response:
Group members will present, through a role play, the truth that enables a person to look to God even when experiencing feelings that lead to despair.

Resource Materials:
___ Bibles
___ one copy of *Can't Fight the Feelings* for each member

HOPE IS ON THE WAY!

❤ HEARTBEAT

☞ [HINT: If you have group members who have been absent the last week or two, asking members to discuss what they have learned about loving others and themselves may provide a good review for everyone. Remember, if you are using follow-through activities, each meeting should begin with or include an evaluation of group members' application of these activities since the last group meeting.]

Learning to love others and ourselves even when we don't feel this love has been our focus in our last two sharing times together. Love for self and others is based on the love we have received from God. In this small group time we will seek God's wisdom and truth in dealing with some extremely painful emotions which may threaten our confidence in God's love for us.

Circumstances and relationships can lead us to feel distant or isolated from the truth of God's love. Without confident security we can be led to despair. Extreme despair can lead a person to believe life is not worth living. Let's take a few minutes to examine the roots of despair.

Johnny's Story

Johnny is 16 years old and an excellent piano and electric keyboard player. He has been taking lessons since he was 7 years old and has always been an eager, disciplined student. His dream in life is to get a college scholarship with his music and become a member of a Christian band. He already has written and performed several Christian songs. Johnny's parents are not very active in the church and are not very supportive of his aspirations to become a Christian musician. However, they have always pushed him to do well in his music because they cannot afford college

CAN'T FIGHT THE FEELINGS

tuition. He has felt more and more pressure from them to do well as he gets closer to graduation from high school.

Recently Johnny's parents have been fighting every night, except for the nights when his dad does not come home. As a result, Johnny has not been able to concentrate. His grades are dropping and he has almost stopped his practicing on the piano. For a month, he has prayed every day that his parents would stop fighting. He cannot bear seeing them like this and his worries over the situation are ruining his studies and music. He worries that he has made things worse by bringing home bad grades and yelling back at his parents when they mentioned his lack of discipline with his music.

Last night, his mother told him she was leaving his dad and that he would have to choose what he would do. She also told him that with the divorce he had better be sure to get his grades up and his music improved because she would have nothing to give him to help him in college.

Johnny is feeling like God has just stopped caring about him. His whole world is falling apart and now his future dreams seem impossible. Johnny wishes he could just disappear.

Johnny is beginning to experience despair. The roots of despair are feelings of worthlessness, helplessness, and hopelessness. Let's look at how these are present in Johnny's life.

ROOT #1: Feelings of Worthlessness. A person has experienced broken relationships or personal failures which lead him to think that he has little or no real self-worth.

What are some things in Johnny's life that could cause him to begin to doubt his self-worth?

HOPE IS ON THE WAY!

ROOT #2: Feelings of Helplessness. A person has experienced loss or hurt or disappointment. The person sees no way out of the problem and feels helpless to do anything which would make a difference.

What are some things in Johnny's life which could cause him to begin to feel out of control and helpless?

ROOT #3: Feelings of Hopelessness. A person views the future situation as one which can only get worse. The person finds no reason to believe that he will successfully work through the circumstances or find healing for the hurt.

What are some things in Johnny's life which could cause him to begin to feel that there is no hope for him?

☞ **[HELP: Some of your group members may themselves have been suicidal at one point or have lost a friend to suicide. Be sensitive to those who feel uncomfortable revealing their experiences in dealing with these issues. Always follow up group members who become unusually silent, cry, display strong emotion, or seem to distance themselves from others during this time.]**

We have all heard and perhaps said things such as "I wish I had never been born." This may just be an emotional outburst because of our momentary feelings of desperation. But the stress and hurt can build up to the point that we begin to feel desperate for extended periods of time. Statements such as "I want to just go away forever" or "I want to kill myself " may become more than emotional outbursts if we do not find hope in periods of desperation.

☞ **[HELP: The depths of despair lead some adolescents to begin to consider suicide. Suicide is, in fact, the number two cause of death among youth. The follow-**

ing warning signals may alert you to young people who are in danger of experiencing life-threatening despair.
1. Sudden behavior changes.
2. Lasting depression
3. Heavy use of drugs or alcohol
4. Insomnia or sleeping too much
5. Comments like "I'd rather be dead"
6. Putting things in final order
7. Withdrawal from family and friends
8. Loss of his/her sense of humor
9. Crying over simple matters
10. Inability to cry even if s/he wants to
11. Difficulty making decisions
12. Seeming overwhelmed by small tasks
13. Loss of appetite

While any of the above symptoms may occur in an adolescent's life as a result of stress, a number of these symptoms combined together constitute major warning signals. How can you intervene in the life of someone who is in a suicidal crisis situation?
1. Be familiar with the danger signals.
2. Trust your judgment.
3. Let others know—do not try to intervene all alone.
4. Stay with a suicidal individual—make sure you are able to get help for the person, but never leave him or her alone until a full intervention has taken place.
5. Listen carefully and empathetically—do not advise or offer spiritual or intellectual reasons why the person should not commit suicide. Your role is to be there, listen, and get help.
6. Encourage professional help.
7. Support the individual by making sure they have the follow-up and resources they need.

From Trinity College Counseling Center Guidelines, Steven Hines and Teresa Dunn.]

HOPE IS ON THE WAY!

Ask group members to share some of the circumstances, from this case study or from their own experience, which would lead someone to the point of genuine despair. Invite — but do not force — personal examples of a time someone they knew went through an extended period of feeling worthless, helpless, or hopeless.

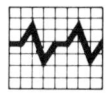

LIFELINE

The Bible reveals to us a number of people who came to the brink of despair before God intervened.

Elijah

Elijah was God's prophet for a great victory over the prophets of Baal. Read about this victory in 1 Kings 18:37-46. Now turn to 1 Kings 19:1-10. Describe how Elijah was feeling here. What seems to have happened?

How did Elijah find his way out of his despair?

☞ [HELP: God sent others to minister to Elijah, those who could care for him, but he had lost sight of them. He felt isolated and helpless until God showed him the provision He had made and would continue to make for him.]

Jonah

Jonah also struggled with despair after a great victory. Read Jonah 4. Describe what had happened and how Jonah felt about it.

☞ [HELP: Jonah felt angry and helpless to get God to do what he wanted. He began to pity himself and think that his life was worthless. Jonah was despairing because he had finally done what God wanted and it did not turn out his way.]

CAN'T FIGHT THE FEELINGS

What evidence do we have of Jonah's response? What options did Jonah have at this point?

☞ **[HELP: It might be helpful to apply the ICE pattern for Jonah's situation. He is an example of someone who got wrapped up in his own agenda and feelings and lost sight of what God was doing in his life. Explore what might have happened if he'd been less self-centered. Help group members see that the key is going to God for worth, help, and hope.]**

God is the God of help, hope, and worth. But even we as His people feel like that help, hope, and worth are far away at times. Our circumstances seem overwhelming. Or someone hurts us in an important relationship. Or maybe we are disappointed, even angry with God because things have not turned out as we expected. The important choice we must make in times of despair is to turn to God, even when we do not feel like doing so.

David
David felt all the feelings of worthlessness, helplessness, and hopelessness. Read the following verses and write out what it was about God that enabled David to find worth, help, and hope.

Worth: Psalm 51:1-17

Hope: Psalm 71:1-6

Help: Psalm 73:21-28

BODYLIFE

Invite your group members to imagine that Johnny is a member of the group. Then role-play helping Johnny ICE his feelings. Begin the role play with one group

member playing Johnny and another being himself or herself. Be sure to let several different group members have a chance at playing the role of the one who talks with Johnny.

☞ [HELP: Remind participants not to just start by telling Johnny what to believe or do. Encourage them to listen, help Johnny understand what he is feeling and why, and apply truth to the choices he has about loving himself and God.

If your group is still inhibited with one another, you may have to play the part of Johnny to help them feel more comfortable.

Also, you will want to recognize that what they say and do in the role play is revealing a part of how they would actually deal with others and themselves when facing despair. You can gain some key insight into the nature of group members' mindsets.]

☞ [HINT: Remember to always debrief after your role plays. Begin with questions which are directed first toward feelings, then personal opinions and values. In this way group members move from observation to affective responses to personal evaluation. Each of these levels increases the depth of vulnerability which it requires from the participants. Generic debriefing questions to be adapted for specific role plays include the following:
- How did you feel when so-and-so said such-and-such?
- Was there a time when your feelings changed toward so-and-so?
- What are your feelings about this issue right now?
- How have these feelings changed or intensified as a result of this role play?
- What were the most important statements which you heard?

- What has happened that is positive in this role play?
- What are some negative things you would be concerned about?
- How would you do this differently if we were to begin again? (Replaying role plays is an excellent technique for discovery learning.)
- What from this role play can be applied to our real-life relationships?]

In order to help one another in this group and others in our lives, we need truth upon which we can base our decisions even when we feel worthless, helpless, and hopeless. Based on the Scripture we have read and discussed, complete these sentences individually. We will then share together our statements of affirmation based on truth.

Life Response
I know I am not worthless because. . . .
I know I am not hopeless because. . . .
I know I am not helpless because. . . .
I can be confident in myself because I belong to God and God is the God of: w _____ , h _____ , and h _____ .

☞ [HELP: This is not a 1-2-3 process which makes everything fine and wonderful. Group members need your support in accepting that working through these feelings is not easy and may take a long time. The important thing to realize is that, because we have a God who gives us worth, help, and hope, we can find victory over despair even when it seems impossible.

It is also important to realize the significant role we play in each others' lives by being human witnesses of the God who is there for us. God has made us to be in relationship with each other in the body of Christ so

HOPE IS ON THE WAY!

that we might experience His love and presence in a very physical presence. Affirm your group members for their potential in making a difference in one anothers' lives in times of despair.

☞ [HELP: Additional optional LIFE RESPONSES:
1. Group members may want to seek further counsel for dealing with despair. Or they may have friends in despair. Be prepared either to be personally available for listening and encouraging group members or to refer them to someone who is willing to fill this role. Do not feel that you need to be a professional counselor, but realize that you can make a difference.
2. Group members may want to do some reading on how to help hurting friends. Check with publishers and your local Christian bookstore for information on how peers can become significant ministers to one another in times of emotional pain. You may want to organize a retreat or seminar to further equip them. Some resources you may find helpful:
- *Counseling Teenagers*, Keith Olson (Group)
- *Equipped to Care: A Youth Worker's Guide to Counseling Teenagers*, William J. Rowley (Victor)
- *Intensive Care*, Rich VanPelt (Zondervan)
- *Training Teenagers for Peer Ministry*, Barbara B. Varenhorst (Group)

3. Group members can commit to spending time with God this week praying for His help and hope in circumstances which currently seem very difficult for them. Encourage group members to pray together and apply the role play to their own circumstances as they support one another in turning to God rather than being overwhelmed by despair.]

What's Next?

"I'm Getting Very Angry"—How can you ICE the hot feelings of anger?

FIVE

▼

I'm Getting Very Angry

SESSION OVERVIEW

Purpose:
In "I'm Getting Very Angry," group members will see the contrast between choosing the human path of retribution as opposed to the biblical pattern of resolution when they find themselves feeling angry. They will practice applying the Identify-Clarify-Exemplify pattern to their angry emotions in order to find resolution as a result of God's presence and power in their lives.

Needs:
Anger can be very difficult to understand. Because it is often such a strong emotion, it is confusing for an adolescent to know what is truly appropriate behavior in response to anger. Some of your group members may even feel guilty for having gotten angry because they think that it is not the "Christian" thing to do. Others cannot seem to gain any control and tend to lash out at those with whom they become upset.

Anger is neutral and natural, but our response to anger can be very dangerous—to ourselves and others. We need

I'M GETTING VERY ANGRY

wisdom and practice in being angry yet not sinning.

Goals:
The *leader's* goals are
(1) to be honest with group members concerning anger;
(2) to guide group members through the process of identifying their own responses to anger;
(3) to provide opportunities for group members to practice appropriate responses to one another in the midst of anger.

The goals for *group members* are that they
(1) adopt the biblical response of seeking resolution for anger by approaching God;
(2) understand the appropriateness of righteous anger;
(3) explore ways of responding to their own anger;
(4) develop an attitude that accepts and expresses anger in a way that will exemplify Christ.

Life Response:
Group members will outline a procedure for dealing with angry emotions which will include a PAST (Personal Anger Support Team).

Resource Materials:
___ Bibles
___ one copy of *Can't Fight the Feelings* for each member

CAN'T FIGHT THE FEELINGS

♥ HEARTBEAT
Read this case study together.

☞ [**HINT: Readings of this length are best done by reading around the circle so that no one gets bored with one voice and everyone keeps up with the material.**]

Melissa has had a terrible, awful, rotten, no-good, very bad day. She remembered when she woke up this morning that she had wanted to skip school. She was certain at that point she could convince her mother to let her stay home, but then she realized that if she stayed home she would not be able to go out with Bruce in the evening. They had a double date set with Dan and Barb, planning to go to a movie, then for pizza, and back home for a late-night ice cream sundae. No way was she going to take a chance on missing this date after she had begged so long to go out on a school night.

"If only I had known then what I know now," she thought to herself, feeling more depressed by the moment. "I never should have gotten out of bed this morning."

When she got to school she realized that she had forgotten her math homework and, more important, the earrings which matched her outfit perfectly. All she could think about all day was getting out of school, going home to change, and then spending the evening with Bruce and their friends away from all the hassles.

The period before she was to meet Bruce for lunch she went to biology class. After one of those gross biology films the teacher handed back the midterm exam grades. What little appetite she had left after the biology film was gone completely when she saw the red ink and the rather

I'M GETTING VERY ANGRY

large, loud "63" which appeared at the top of the paper.

"Wonderful!" she said to herself, though loudly enough for others to hear as well. Her day may not have been a lot of things so far, but it was certainly consistent.

At lunch Bruce told her that his mother had grounded him because he had not been doing his work around the house as he had promised. He had to cancel tonight's date.

Melissa was so mad by that point that she could not even talk to Bruce. She just ate three bites of lunch and said, "See you tomorrow, unless you're grounded from school too!" She knew that she should not be so rude, but she was mad and he was only making it worse. Part of her felt bad and the rest of her just did not care anymore.

By the time she got home all she wanted was to be left alone. She went to her room, closed the door, and turned the stereo on—LOUD! Unfortunately, she did not know her mother was taking a nap upstairs. Her mother, of course, very specifically informed her of this fact within moments.

When Pamela called at 7:00 and asked Melissa to meet her for yogurt and to pick up some things for her mother, Melissa decided that it might help her mood if she could get out of the house. "At least," she reasoned, "it can't get any worse."

As Pamela and Melissa came out with their yogurt they saw Bruce standing in the parking lot! What was worse was that he was standing next to his car, talking and laughing with Allison, his ex-girlfriend!

Melissa could not believe it. "Grounded, huh?" she shouted to Pamela, loud enough for Bruce to hear. She moved

CAN'T FIGHT THE FEELINGS

quickly toward the car shouting to Pamela, "I'll ground him!"

Bruce heard her and started to come toward her. Melissa said, "Let's just go, Pamela. I never want to see him again!" With this, they left Bruce standing in the parking lot yelling, "Wait! Where are you going, Melissa?"

So here is Melissa nearing the end of the terrible, awful, rotten, no-good, very bad day. She is getting angrier by the moment on the way home with Pamela.

Pamela asks, "What are you going to do now, Melissa?" but Melissa shrugs her shoulders. Right now she just wishes she had an umbrella. It is a long walk from the street to her front door, and it is just starting to rain really hard.

In groups of three, write out your answers to the following questions:

1. Describe what you think Melissa would be feeling.

2. How is Melissa dealing with her feelings?

3. What would you say to Melissa if you were Pamela?

4. If you were Melissa, what would you want Pamela to do?

5. What options does Melissa have in terms of dealing with her emotions at this point?

6. Honestly, what would you do if you were Melissa?

Allow the smaller groups several minutes to complete their discussions. Then engage the whole group in giving feedback to the questions.

I'M GETTING VERY ANGRY

After this is completed, inform the students that you just happen to have "The Rest of the Story," which might be helpful to know if you were Melissa or Melissa's friend, Pamela. Here is the rest of the story:

Bruce called Pamela later that night to ask what he should do. He knew Melissa was very upset. However, he also knew that he had not done anything wrong. He truly was grounded and his mom had sent him to the grocery store for some milk. It was there he stopped for a moment to talk to Allison. He spoke to her for only a few moments and was not in any way flirting with her. Unfortunately, it was one of those few moments that Melissa and Pamela had seen. He could verify his story if Melissa would listen to his mother or Allison. For now, he did not know what to do.

Ask group members, "If Bruce is really telling the truth, how would this change Melissa's feelings?"

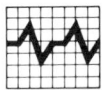

LIFELINE

Divide into "cell groups" of two or three to examine a family in the Old Testament who was living out what sounds like a plot to a modern television soap opera. Work through this study of Joseph's less-than-happy home in preparation for a discussion on how to deal with anger.

Hebrew "Dallas"

1. Review the Relationships

Read Genesis 37. After you have read the verses, briefly describe the following relationships within the family.
   a. Joseph/Father:
   b. Joseph/Brothers:
   c. Brothers/Father:
   d. Joseph/Reuben:
   e. Joseph/Judah:
   f. Reuben/Brothers:
   g. Judah/Brothers:

2. Examine the Facts
   a. How old was Joseph?
   b. What did his two dreams mean?
   c. What did Joseph's brothers do to him?

3. Understand Hurt and Anger in the Family
   a. Joseph's brothers
      - They were angry and hurt because. . . .
      - They dealt with these feelings by. . . .
   b. Joseph's Father
      - He was hurt and angry because. . . .
      - He dealt with these feelings by. . . .
   c. Joseph
      - How do you think Joseph must have been feeling during the events of Genesis 37?
      - What possible choices could Joseph have made to deal with these feelings?

☞ **[HELP: As you discuss with the group the choices facing Joseph, help them evaluate what took place among the brothers. The brothers were not just angry at Joseph, they were also very angry at their father. Further study into this family reveals that there was a lot of hurt and bitterness about the way the father favored Joseph and later Benjamin.**

The brothers chose RETRIBUTION. They hurt Joseph and their father to get even. The father was in such mourning at his loss that he was facing DESTITUTION, as if life were over. Joseph could have taken either of these routes. Instead, he chose RESOLUTION, for what must have been a lot of hurt and anger, as group members will discover in Genesis 45.]

Let's look at Joseph's choice as it is revealed in Genesis 45:1-7. What had he done to deal with his anger?

☞ **[HELP: You may want to review Joseph's attitude**

when he was first enslaved, his attitude in Potiphar's house, and his attitude while in prison. Joseph did not give in to any feelings of self-pity, nor did he harbor bitterness and hate. He resolved his anger by trusting God.]

Christian Anger?

Let's read Ephesians 4:26-27. We do not have to think we are sinful whenever we get angry. What is sinful is when we choose to deal with our anger on our own terms, taking it out on ourselves or others, rather than taking it to God for resolution. It's the angry choice that gets us into problems, not the anger itself.

BODYLIFE

Fill out the first three questions in the "Anger Survey" in preparation for a group discussion on how we deal with our anger.

Anger Survey

1. When I am very upset, I . . .
   a. become very quiet.
   b. talk it out.
   c. take it out on my brother/sister.
   d. yell or curse.
   e. pretend I don't care.
   f. eat and eat.
   g. exercise to reduce stress.
   h. Other:

2. I think that anger is . . .
   a. no big deal.
   b. scary.
   c. better than being bored.
   d. hard to express.
   e. OK—if you control it.

f. wrong.
g. the hardest emotion for me.
h. sometimes pleasing to God.
i. never pleasing to God.
j. Other:

3. When Christians get angry, they should _____ because....

☞ [HINT: Dividing the discussion allows for the building of trust in the first three, less personal questions, in preparation for a deeper vulnerability on the tougher questions of 4–7. Be sure to discuss the first three thoroughly and then continue.]

4. One thing I would change about myself or my actions when I get angry is....

5. I have been very hurt by someone else's anger when he/she . . .
   a. was not honest about it.
   b. took it out on me.
   c. seemed angry for no reason.
   d. ruined a friendship.
   e. took it out on my friend.
   f. let it change them.
   g. Other:

6. It is usually the most difficult for me to deal with my anger when....

7. My most common responses to anger in situations like numbers 5 and 6, when I am very hurt and angry, are....

☞ [HINT: You may want to use a follow-through question to help group members clarify the reasons for the way they act when they are angry. Is it because they learned this from a parent? Is it because it feels the safest? Is it because they are afraid no one will listen if they do not behave this way?]

When the anger is heating up, you will want to control the emotions by taking time to ICE them down. Doing so will help you make decisions of the will based on God's truth rather than decisions of the emotions based on your circumstances.

☞ [HINT: As the leader you want to be sensitive to students sharing very painful feelings or episodes. Be certain that you communicate your appreciation of their honesty and their willingness to be vulnerable. You are, in effect, modeling the ICE pattern of dealing with emotions by helping them identify their anger and the reason for the ways they usually respond.]

Life Response

With the help of your friends in this group, write out a procedure which you will attempt to follow when the anger starts to boil. Include in this procedure a PAST (Personal Anger Support Team) that you can turn to when you feel your emotional temperature rising in anger. This PAST can help you talk through your feelings, getting you past the anger and into a clear perspective on how God can help you find a resolution.

When I get angry, I will. . . .

☞ [HELP: A number of practical methods can work to reduce anger. Counting to 25 before speaking, working out or exercising, listening to soothing music, reading a pleasant book, and many other activities can help individuals begin to cool down. Ultimately, final resolution requires taking the feelings to God and to others to process through them and come to terms with the source of the anger.

In some instances coming to terms means making changes, while in other instances it means accepting that certain things are beyond our control and we have to trust God with them.]

☞ [HELP: The best possible additional LIFE RESPONSE for this learning experience would be to have students keep a record of when they had to use the procedure they just outlined, including their PAST, so that you can come together to talk about its effectiveness in resolving anger.]

What's Next?

"Crowd Control" — How do you react when the crowd turns on you?

SIX
▼

Crowd Control

SESSION OVERVIEW

Purpose:
"Crowd Control" completes *Can't Fight the Feelings* with a look at the role of our emotions in the decision-making process. Group members will explore how individuals and groups can be very fickle when they rely on their emotions as their primary guide. In this sharing time they will apply the understanding and insight they have gained the last few weeks to living lives which accept and work with personal feelings rather than fighting them or allowing them to control us. Special attention will be given to peer pressure.

Needs:
Adolescents can be a bundle of changing, churning emotions. Some display this outwardly, while others keep the tension either neatly wrapped or desperately stuffed inside. Your group members need to be able to express their emotions in ways that exemplify Christ.

To do so, they must begin to practice self-control—not because emotions are bad but because emotions are not a test of truth.

CAN'T FIGHT THE FEELINGS

You can help your group members see that they can be proactive rather than reactive by not making decisions based on their emotions, especially when those emotions are being influenced by others. Since peer pressure lives off the fear of being rejected and desire to be loved, the ability to understand *what* we are feeling and *why* is a tremendous resource in the struggle to not give in to the crowd.

Goals:
The *leader's* goals include
(1) guiding group members to a healthy perspective on the role of emotions in their lives;
(2) assisting group members in their evaluation of how the media and peers can influence emotions;
(3) enabling group members to confront their own need to make decisions based on the truth of God's Word;
(4) facilitating a closure to the group which will support continued growth together in their small group relationships.

Goals for the *group members* are that they
(1) understand the fickle nature of emotions;
(2) evaluate the influence of peers on their emotions;
(3) develop a plan for decision-making when emotions are strong;
(4) commit to continued relationships of accountability with others in the matter of emotions.

Life Response:
Each group member will share one or two specific ways in which he or she needs the support of Christian peers to learn to ICE emotions and not give in to peer pressure.

Resource Materials:
___ Bibles
___ sentences and container for the BODYLIFE activity
___ one copy of *Can't Fight the Feelings* for each member

♡ HEARTBEAT

A once-famous television commercial slogan said, "Try it, you'll like it." Commercials are designed to convince you that you have a need that should be met and that particular product or service can best meet your personal need.

In "cell groups" of two or three, list as many television commercials as you can think of that try to arouse an emotional reaction in order to sell you on their product or service. Beside each commercial write the emotion they want you to experience, such as happiness or sadness or excitement, in order to gain your allegiance to the product.

☞ **[HELP: This activity is designed to help group members evaluate how emotions can be used to persuade, in some cases to the point of manipulation.]**

What would happen if you always responded to the emotions you felt when watching commercials?

☞ **[HELP: Emotions are a part of making decisions and must not be ignored. Neither, however, should these emotions become the bases of decisions.]**

A very popular cultural motto of a few years ago stated, "If it feels good, do it!" Would you agree or disagree with that statement? Explain your view.

We have been applying the Identify-Clarify-Exemplify pattern in our previous group times. As we have seen, emotions are natural and neutral. The key is our making responsible choices based on truth rather than just going with our feelings. In this final group time we will examine how individuals and groups can make very destructive decisions when they are not choosing based on what is true. We will also see how important the support of Christian friends can be when we have to make decisions that do not feel good at the moment.

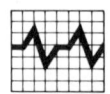

LIFELINE

Let's begin by dividing into two smaller groups. Group A will read and discuss Luke 19:28-38. Group B will read and discuss Luke 23:13-25.

After you have read these passages, answer the following questions:

- How was the crowd feeling toward Jesus?

- How were they treating Him?

- Why do you think they were treating Him this way?

☞ [HELP: These passages examine how the same crowd turned from praising Jesus to condemning Him to death. The rise of the crowd's feelings swept up almost everyone in fear, anger, and hate. The crowd's negative reaction to Jesus produced a mass evil beyond what we can imagine as they yelled, "Crucify Him!" at the Son of God.

Leaders' manipulation and the peer pressure by members of a crowd have incredibly devastating potential. On a much smaller scale your group members have probably seen the results of emotional crowd pressure.]

As a total group, let's consider this question:

What types of emotions do your peers feel when they are experiencing peer pressure?

☞ **[HELP: Peer pressure capitalizes on the need to be loved and accepted and the parallel fear of rejection. People who feel especially negative about themselves or lonely are least prepared to deal with such pressure.]**

Give an example, perhaps from your own experience, of a time when pressure from the crowd led someone to change his behavior or attitudes.

Self-control Beats Crowd Control
God has provided His Spirit in our lives as the power we need to overcome crowd control. Galatians 5:23 tells us that part of the result of having God's Spirit is that we can have self-control. Second Timothy 1:7 states, "God did not give us a spirit of timidity, but a spirit of power, of love and of self-discipline."

In other words, while we may experience the emotions that come with peer pressure, we do not have to give in to those feelings because we have a greater source of control in our lives: His Spirit of truth.

BODYLIFE
All of us need times to talk about our emotions, to identify what is going on, and to seek help for making good decisions. Other people can provide objective viewpoints which help us clarify what is happening. In this way we are better able to get beyond our immediate emotional responses and focus on the wisdom and strength we need from God's Spirit within us.

Facts before Feelings
Imagine a train whose engine is labeled "FACTS" and whose caboose is labeled "FEELINGS." If the train is not pulled along by its engine as it attempts to climb a hill, the

caboose will pull it back down. If, however, the engine is functioning well, the whole train moves forward, pulling the caboose along with it.

Overcoming the uphill climb against peer pressure works in a similar way. If we are being "driven" by the facts, we can move forward and our feelings will follow along. But it often takes working through our emotions, as we have experienced with the ICE pattern, to be able to clearly see the truth.

Staying on Track
These past few meetings have been dedicated to teaching us how to help one another "stay on track" during times of emotional changes and stress. Let's take some time to talk together about what we have experienced together in this series of small group sharing meetings.

☞ [HELP: This is the same activity as the opening exercise found in session 1. Organize this activity in the same way, using a container with the 10 slips of paper placed inside. Remember, the first round is simply responding to the statement while round two includes active discussion among the group. The statements this time are much more personal and reflect the experiences that students have been having together in the small group meetings.

Here are 10 suggested statements (you may want to write your own if your group has different issues which would be helpful to discuss):

1. An emotion which is difficult for me to experience or express is. . . .
2. A time when I have felt very angry was. . . .
3. A time when I have felt very loved was. . . .
4. How I have been feeling about someone in this group recently is. . . .
5. How I have been feeling about myself recently is. . . .
6. How I have been feeling toward God recently is. . . .
7. How I feel when I am around a crowd which I know wants me to be different or act differently before they will accept me is. . . .
8. Some of the feelings I have about my closest friends are. . . .
9. Ways in which this group has helped me feel better about myself are. . . .
10. Lately I've been feeling . . . about my life.]

Life Response

Let's close our series of meetings together by having each one of us complete the sentence listed below and then discussing our answers together.

"When I am struggling with my emotions or with pressures from the crowd, Christian friends can support me by. . . ."

☞ [HELP: Possible additional optional LIFE REPONSES to this series:
1. Group members may want to commit to continuing to meet together and beginning another topical series with this small group.
2. Group members may want to extend this series for another meeting or two to ask some more questions or get some more information on dealing with emotions.

3. Group members may want to commit to a training program which would prepare them to be peer counselors so that they can minister to their hurting friends. (See the list of resources at the end of session 4.)

4. Group members may want to commit to be available to one another when they are facing tough emotions and need someone to talk with as they try to apply the ICE pattern.

5. Group members may want to join you in preparing to help lead another small group through this material. In this way students would be developing discipling skills as they work with you.]

LEADER'S EVALUATION SHEET
Can't Fight the Feelings

Please take a minute to fill out and mail this form giving us your candid reaction to this material. Thanks for your help!

In what setting did you use this Small Group Study? (Sunday School, youth group, midweek Bible study, etc.)

How many young people were in your group? _____

What was the age range of those in your group? _____

How long was your average meeting? _____

Do you plan to use other SonPower Small Group Studies? _____ Why or why not?

Did you and your young people enjoy this study? Why or why not?

What are the strengths and/or weaknesses of this leader's edition?

What are the strengths and/or weaknesses of the student book?

Would you like more information on SonPower Youth Sources?

Name	_____
Church name	_____
Church address	_____
	_____
Church phone	(_____)_____
Church size	_____

SGY02

PLACE
STAMP
HERE

**SonPower Youth Sources Editor
Victor Books
1825 College Avenue
Wheaton, Illinois 60187**